USING GOD'S WORD TO GUIDE IN PRAYING FOR THE BIG ISSUES IN OUR WORLD

Praying for Big Things

ADDICTION AND THE OPIOID CRISIS
ILLNESS, LOSS, PAIN OR DEPRESSION
LEADERSHIP
MIGRANT, PERSECUTED, AND REFUGEE COMMUNITIES
NATURAL DISASTERS
RACISM AND PREJUDICE
SEXUAL ABUSE AND PORNOGRAPHY
VIOLENCE, TERRORISM, AND WAR

Leoma G. Gilley

2nd Edition

Cover and book design: Howell Graphics

Unless otherwise indicated, all Scripture quotations are taken from the Holy Bible, New Living Translation, copyright © 1996, 2004, 2007, 2013, 2015 by Tyndale House Foundation. Used by permission of Tyndale House Publishers, Inc., Carol Stream, Illinois 60188. All rights reserved.

© 2017 by Leoma G. Gilley
2nd Edition © 2020 Leoma G. Gilley

ALL RIGHTS RESERVED. Reproduction of the whole or any part of the contents without written permission is prohibited.

Library of Congress Control Number: 2020924027

ISBN: 978-1-970037-562   Praying for BIG Things

Printed in the United States of America

Dedication

To Pam Bendor-Samuel

You inspired me to think about praying
for the big issues of our world.

Acknowledgments

I want to thank the staff and congregation of All Souls, Langham Place, London for their support and encouragement. Their willingness to launch the original edition of this book was a great incentive and confirmation.

Thanks to those who have contributed ideas and verses for prayer. Special thanks go to Rev. Clay Harrington for his helpful comments and suggestions to improve the first edition of this book. I'm grateful to Jody Dyer and Jan Camburn for their editing of the current book. Any errors that remain are the responsibility of the author.

Many thanks to Harriet Howell for typesetting this book even with all the changes I made after she started.

I've made use of Quick Verse, a Bible program. Quick Verse Version 3.0.0 of FindEx.com, Inc.

The prayers produced in this book were inspired by five versions of the Bible, including Holy Bible, New Living Translation; The Message: The Bible in Contemporary Language; The Holy Bible, New Century Version; God's Word; and The Holy Bible, English Standard Version.

Table of Contents

Introduction	6
Addiction and the Opioid Crises	8
Illness, Loss, Pain or Depression	16
Leadership	35
A. Government, Business, Education	36
B. Religious Leaders	45
C. Congregations	51
D. Pastoral Search Team	55
Migrant, Persecuted and Refugee Communities	60
Natural Disasters	80
Racism and Prejudice	89
Sexual Abuse and Pornography	96
Violence, Terrorism and War	104
Topical Index	119
References	124

Introduction

There are many books about prayer, and there are books of prayers. This book is a book of prayers inspired by scripture. Having been challenged many years ago to learn how to pray for situations that were too big, too damaging, too vast for me to know how to pray, I felt I needed help and that God's own words would be the best guide I could find. I have lived in a country that has undergone more than twenty years of a brutal civil war. I have friends who have lost loved ones in battle and from illness, who have been separated from their families for years, not knowing if their relatives were dead or alive. I've seen bad leaders and great leaders, witnessed mass migrations of people, and worked with refugees. I have friends and loved ones who have died or are dying from cancer. As this second edition is published, we are living through the COVID-19 pandemic and serious racial tensions. How do we bring these very real problems into our prayers?

As I considered this question, verses of scripture seemed to jump out at me almost saying, "Pray me!" So, that is how the writing of this book began. It doesn't cover everything, but it is a beginning, and I hope it will help to enrich and deepen your prayer life as it has mine.

In writing this book, I've had to confront this question: what is the purpose of prayer? Discussing with God the issues that are on our hearts when we watch the news or talk with people in distress can draw us closer to God's heart. That coming together helps us grow in relationship with the triune God. Our awareness and engagement in the issues in our world also help us recognize when these situations change. We see God's hand at work, and we can give him praise.

We know from Romans 8:26-27, "In the same way, the Spirit helps us in our weakness. We do not know what we ought to pray for, but the Spirit himself intercedes for us through wordless groans. [27] And he who searches our hearts knows the mind of the Spirit, because the Spirit intercedes for God's people in accordance with the will of God." (NIV)." So, thankfully, it is not up to us to "get it right." The Spirit does that for us. So, what is the purpose? God knows what is needed and is working all things out for his good. He asks us to join him and be amazed at what he does. Then we can offer our wonder, love, and praise.

As the scripture tells us: "Devote yourselves to prayer with an alert mind and a thankful heart." (Colossians 4:2)

Addiction and the Opioid Crisis

Addictions come in many forms: drugs, alcohol, pornography. All of them lead to the destruction of individuals, families and communities.

Addiction

*B*e gracious to those caught up in addiction, O God, for pain and desire hound addicts; all day long their addiction oppresses them; those wanting to sell them drugs pursue them without a break.

When they are afraid, may they put their trust in you, O God, whose word does not fail; help them not to be afraid.

Do you see what other people are doing to those trying to get free from this bondage? The dealers and other addicts don't let up—they smear their reputations and huddle to plot for the addict's collapse. They gang up and sneak together through the alleys to take their victims by surprise, waiting for their chance to get them.

For these actions will you allow them to escape? Take on these evil people, O God!

You have kept count of the sleepless nights and put their tears in your bottle. Aren't their sorrows and suffering recorded in your book? Enter each of their aches and pains in your ledger. When they call for help, cause their enemies to run away. May they be confident that you, God, are on their side.

We praise you, God, for what you have promised; yes, we praise you, LORD, that you are faithful to do as you have promised. Keep them trusting in God so they will not be afraid. Then what can mere mortals do to them?

Enable them to fulfill their vows to you, O God, and to give you their thank offerings. Deliver souls from death and keep their feet from slipping so that they may walk in your presence and in your life-giving light.

LORD, in your mercy, hear our prayer.

Based on Psalm 56

Confession

LORD, may those who have been addicted to any harmful thing know the joy that comes when their sins have been forgiven and wiped away. May these addicts confess their failures to you without trying to hide them and thus know your cleansing. Help them to live lives of complete honesty.

Remind them how it felt when they refused to confess their sins: their bodies wasting away, groaning all day long. Your hand of discipline weighed heavily on them until their strength was nearly gone, evaporating like water in the summer heat.

May they confess all their sins to you and stop trying to

hide their guilt and failures. Then they can know that you have put things right and taken away their guilt, and they won't be subject to your judgment. Instead, you will be their hiding place, protecting them from trouble. Surround them with songs of victory. Point out the road that they should follow. Be their teacher and guide who watches over them on this new path of freedom from addiction.

There is plenty of trouble for those who choose the path of wickedness, but your kindness shields those who trust in you, LORD. So, as these addicts choose to put their trust and confidence in you, may they find occasion to celebrate and shout with joy.

LORD, in your mercy, hear our prayer.

Based on Psalm 32

Children

*L*ORD, we pray for the children who are impacted by the addictions of their parents, whether those addictions are drugs, alcohol, pornography, or patterns of abuse. We pray for the protection of those children because you have told us that if anyone causes one of these little ones who trusts in you to fall into sin, it would be better for that person to be thrown into the sea with a millstone tied around his or her neck and left to drown. Bring those who can rescue these children from danger so the children will be able to live in safety.

LORD, in your mercy, hear our prayer.

Based on Matthew 18:6

Decisions

*I*n these days when so much evil is around us, help people not to make foolish decision but ones that are wise. Help them make the most of every opportunity by not acting thoughtlessly but discovering what you, LORD, want them to do. May they not be filled with alcohol or drugs or visual perversions that will ruin their lives. Instead, may they be filled with the Holy Spirit, singing psalms and hymns and spiritual songs, making music to the LORD in their hearts.

LORD, in your mercy, hear our prayer.

Based on Ephesians 5:15-19

Freedom

Have mercy on those caught up by addiction, O God, have mercy! May they and their families look to you for protection. Help them to hide beneath the shadow of your wings until the danger of temptation has passed by. We cry out to God Most High, who has promised to fulfill his purposes for those seeking to be free of addiction. Send help from heaven to rescue them, disgracing those who provide for their addiction.

My God, send your unfailing love and faithfulness to those who want to be free from addiction. They are surrounded by evil influences and people who would greedily devour them like human prey—whose teeth pierce like spears and arrows and whose tongues cut like swords.

Be exalted, O God, above the highest heavens! May your glory shine over all the earth. Their enemies have set a trap for them. They are weary from distress. Evil people have dug deep pits in their paths. Please cause the evil ones to fall into them.

My heart is confident in you, O God; cause addicts' hearts to be confident as well. No wonder I can sing your praises! Wake up, my heart! Wake up, O lyre and harp!
I will wake the dawn with my song. I will thank you, LORD, among all the people. I will sing your praises among the nations. May your love reach higher than the heavens; your loyalty extend beyond the clouds to those seeking to be free from addiction. May they honor you, my God, above the heavens. May your glory be seen everywhere on earth.

LORD, in your mercy, hear our prayer.

Based on Psalm 57

Perpetrators

LORD, we recognize there are people who have thought acknowledging you was foolish, so you abandoned them to their foolish thinking and let them do things that should never be done. Some of these people have pushed inappropriate drugs to doctors so that patients become addicted. Some have taken advantage of women and even young girls to create pornography. Some have encouraged excessive drinking to those with a tendency to addiction. Many have done these things because of greed and love of money. As a result, their lives have become full of every kind of wickedness, sin, greed, hate, envy, murder, quarreling, deception, malicious behavior, and gossip. They hate you and are insolent, proud, and boastful. They even invent new ways of sinning and refuse to follow any authority or law. They refuse to understand the implications of their actions, break their promises, are heartless, and have no mercy. They know what they are doing is wrong, but they do it anyway. What's worse, they encourage others to do them too.

LORD, stop them in their tracks. Bring justice and punish these people who destroy others without pity.

LORD, in your mercy, hear our prayer.

Based on Romans 1:28-32

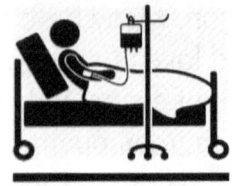

Illness, Loss, Pain, or Depression

Illnesses such as cancer, HIV/AIDS, or COVID-19, addiction, and depression or other psychological issues have significant effects not only on the individual but also on family and friends. Financial stresses, as well as the distress that pain can cause, add to, and compound the problems people face. Let us lift up those in need to the LORD, our Healer, who cares deeply about each one.

Abandonment

*L*ORD, we pray for those who feel they have been abandoned by friends, family, spouse, or children; perhaps, even by you. Cause these lonely ones to be strong and courageous. Help them not to be afraid or to panic when confronted with challenges and troubles. May they see that you go before your people, and have promised to be with them. LORD, we know that you will neither fail nor abandon those who love you and reach out to you.

LORD, in your mercy, hear our prayer.

Based on Deuteronomy 31:6

Brokenhearted

*L*ORD, hear your people when they call out for help, and rescue them from all their troubles. Be close to the brokenhearted and save those whose spirits have been crushed. People have many problems, but you, LORD, are able to solve them all. Protect them...body, mind and soul...and bring healing and wholeness.

LORD, in your mercy, hear our prayer.

Based on Psalm 34:17-20

Darkness

*L*ORD, we pray for those who sit in gloom and darkness like prisoners suffering in chains. They stumble along the way, perhaps rebelling against your words, and no one helps them. In their misery when they cry out to you, LORD, save them from all their troubles. Bring them out of their gloom and darkness and break their chains. Then let them give praise to you, LORD, for your love and for the miracles you do for people. Break their bonds, no matter how solid or how strong.

LORD, in your mercy, hear our prayer.

Based on Psalm 107:10-16

Danger

*L*ORD, we pray for those in dangerous situations. Be their protection wherever they are. Never let your people be put to shame. Save and rescue those in danger; listen to their cries and save them. Be the place of safety where they can always come. Give the command to save them. You are their rock and their strong, walled city. O God, save your people from the power of the wicked and from the hold of the cruel and unjust.

LORD, in your mercy, hear our prayer.

Based on Psalm 71:1-4

Despair

O LORD, we cry out to you for those in the depths of despair. Help them! Hear their cry. Pay attention to their pleas for mercy. LORD, if you kept a record of sins, who could ever survive? But you offer forgiveness so that we might learn to fear you. Those in despair are counting on you; yes, we are all counting on you. We are waiting for your help, more than sentries who long for the dawn, yes, more than watchmen who wait for sunrise.

O LORD, may those in despair find hope in you, for with you there is unlimited forgiveness. Rescue us all from every kind of trouble.

LORD, in your mercy, hear our prayer.

Based on Psalm 130

Disasters

$\mathcal{L}$ORD, we pray for people who are suffering, who seek to live in the shelter of the Most High, and find rest in the shadow of the Almighty, for you alone are their refuge, their place of safety. Rescue your people from every trap and protect them from every deadly disease. Help them not to be afraid of the terrors of the night, or of the dread disease that stalks in darkness, nor the disaster that strikes at midday. Though a thousand fall at their side, though ten thousand are dying around them, don't let these evils touch them. If they make you, the LORD, their refuge, if they make you, the Most High, their shelter, let no evil conquer them, no plague come near their home.

LORD, in your mercy, hear our prayer.

Based on Psalm 91:1-3, 5-7, 9-10

Discouragement

$\mathcal{L}$ORD, we pray for those who are deeply discouraged and sad. May they put their hope in you. Let there be times of rejoicing and praise once more. May there soon be a time when they will be able to praise their Savior and their God. When they hear the tumult of life raging about them, feeling the waves of despair and the surging tides of hopelessness sweeping over them, may they remember that your love is unfailing and that you are present. Through each dark night, may they begin to sing your songs and pray to you, the God who gives life. May they put their hope in you.

LORD, in your mercy, hear our prayer.

Based on Psalm 42:5-8

Elderly

LORD, we pray for the elderly who have depended on you since they were born and have been such examples to us. You have helped them since the days of their births. May they continue to praise and honor you all day long. Help us not to reject them when they are old or desert them when their strength is gone.

LORD, in your mercy, hear our prayer.

Based on Psalm 71:5-9

Endurance

*L*ORD, we pray for those who seem to waver between life and death because of their suffering. They want to be free of their pain and weakness! Can the dead live again? We know this is so; therefore, give them hope through all their sufferings so they can eagerly await release from their pain. Call them home in your time and help them answer your invitation, for you yearn for them, your handiwork, to dwell with you forever. O LORD God, guard their steps.

LORD, in your mercy, hear our prayer.

Based on Job 14:13-17

Faithfulness

*L*ORD, today we pray for those who are filled with misery, to whom you have given a bitter cup of sorrow to drink. We pray for those who may have given up on life altogether and have forgotten what a good life is like. We pray for those whose strength is gone, who have lost hope in you. Remember, O LORD, their suffering, misery, sorrow and trouble. Remember them and think about them, LORD. Enable them to dare to have hope in you and to remember that your faithful love never ends! Your mercies never cease. Great is your faithfulness; your mercies begin afresh each morning. Be good to those who hope in you, to those who search for you.

LORD, in your mercy, hear our prayer.

Based on Lamentations 3:15, 17-23, 25

Fear

LORD, may all who are afraid wait quietly before you and remember that their hope is in you. You alone are their rock and salvation, their defender who cannot be defeated. Remind the fearful that victory and honor come from you alone, O God. You are their refuge, a fortress no enemy can enter.

LORD, in your mercy, hear our prayer.

Based on Psalm 62:5-7

Freedom

LORD, free the anxious from all that they fear. Cause those who look to you for help to be radiant with joy. Never let their faces be covered with shame. When desperate people call to you, LORD, please listen; save them from all their fears. Assign angels as guards to surround and defend all who respect you. Cause these desperate ones to examine and see that you, the LORD, are good. May they find the joys of those who take refuge in you!

LORD, in your mercy, hear our prayer.

Based on Psalm 34:4-8

Generosity

LORD, in order to be the community of believers you want us to be, we should share food with the hungry and welcome poor and homeless people into our homes. We, your people, should give clothes to those who need them and not hide from those who need help... LORD, keep us, your people, from making trouble for others, from using cruel words, and from pointing our fingers at those less fortunate. Instead, help us to feed those who are hungry and take care of the needs of those who are troubled. Help us to be your light, bright like the noon-day sun, shining in the darkness.

LORD, in your mercy, hear our prayer.

Based on Isaiah 58:7, 9-10

God's love

*L*ORD, we pray that Christ will be more and more at home in the hearts of those with serious illness and pain as they trust in you. May they be strong and grounded in your love for them, and may they have the strength, powered by the Holy Spirit, to comprehend how wide, long, high, and deep your love really is. May they experience the love of Christ as fully as possible in this life, even though it is so great they will never fully understand it. Then, fill them with the fullness of life and power that come only from you. By your mighty power, work within them to accomplish more than we or they would ever dare to ask or imagine.

LORD, in your mercy, hear our prayer.

Based on Ephesians 3:17-20

Good Shepherd

*L*ORD, you are the good Shepherd; thank you for providing all that we need. Help those who are weary, tired, and in pain to rest in the lush meadows and beside the peaceful, quiet pools that you offer. May they catch their breath, renew their strength, and be guided in the right paths so that they may bring honor to your name. Remind them that even when they walk through the darkest valley, they don't need to be afraid, for you are always close beside them.

LORD, in your mercy, hear our prayer.

Based on Psalm 23:1-4

Hope

*L*ORD, we pray for your children who grow weary in their present bodies and who long for the day when they will put on their heavenly bodies like new clothing. Assure them they will not be spirits without bodies, but they will put on new, heavenly bodies. Their dying bodies make them groan and sigh. They want to slip into their new bodies so that these dying bodies will be swallowed up by everlasting life. God, you have prepared them for this, and as a guarantee you have given them your Holy Spirit. Cause our suffering friends who would rather be away from these bodies of death to be confident in you, knowing that when they depart this world, they will be at home with you, LORD.

LORD, in your mercy, hear our prayer.

Based on 2 Corinthians 5:2-8

Protection

𝓛ORD, there are many needing your help in so many ways during these days of isolation and illness. Where does our help come from if not from you? You made heaven and earth, so help us not to stumble in our faith or calling. You are not asleep during this crisis. Keep watch over your people. Stand as our protective barrier to disease. Keep us from all harm and watch over our lives. Especially keep watch over those who must come and go to keep them from harm, both now and forever.

LORD, in your mercy, hear our prayer.

Based on Psalm 121

Provision

LORD, give justice to the oppressed and food
to the hungry.
LORD, free the innocent prisoners
and give sight to the blind.
LORD, straighten the backs of those who are bent over
with too many worries and cares.
LORD, we know you love the godly.
LORD, protect the foreigners among us.
LORD, give relief to the orphans and widows,
LORD, frustrate the plans of the wicked.
May you, LORD, reign forever.

LORD, in your mercy, hear our prayer.

Based on Psalm 146:7-10

Restoration

O Sovereign LORD, search for and take care of those who have lost their way. We pray that, like a shepherd, you will look for your scattered people. Find the wandering ones and save them, even from all the places to which they are driven by the dark circumstances they face. Bring them back from far off places to their own land where they can once again find refreshment and support. Work in them so they find true peace.

LORD, in your mercy, hear our prayer.

Based on Ezekiel 34:11-13, 15

Reliance

LORD, we pray for those who feel crushed and overwhelmed beyond their ability to endure and who think they might not live through their current circumstances. In fact, they may expect to die. Help them to use this oppression to stop relying on themselves and start relying only on you, God, who raise the dead. Rescue them from mortal danger and continue to rescue them as the need arises.

LORD, in your mercy, hear our prayer.

Based on 2 Corinthians 1:8-10

Rescue

*L*ORD, you said you would rescue those who love you and protect those who know you. When they call on you, please answer; be with them in trouble. Rescue and honor them. Reward them with long lives and give them your salvation.

LORD, in your mercy, hear our prayer.

Based on Psalm 91:14-16

Restoration

*W*ho can compare with you, O God? You have allowed many to undergo so many hardships, troubles, and bad times, but we ask you to restore them to life again and lift them up from the depths of the earth. Restore them to an even more productive life and comfort them once more.

LORD, in your mercy, hear our prayer.

Based on Psalm 71:19-21

Safety

*L*ORD, in the midst of all that is going on right now, we feel as if we are in a storm at sea: tossed to the heavens one moment only to be plunged to the depths the next. We cringe in terror and are at our wits' end. We cry out to you, "LORD, HELP!" We are trusting that you will save us from our distress, calm this storm raging about us, and bring us to a place of safety and peace. When that happens, may we remember to give you the praise and honor that you deserve.

LORD, in your mercy, hear our prayer.

Based on Psalm 107:23-32

Seekers

*L*ORD, help those who have lost your way to stop at life's crossroads and look around. Remind them to seek the old, godly way, and walk in it; for if they travel that path, they will find rest for their souls. Forgive them when they decide that your way is not the road they want! In the midst of their rush to find satisfaction, help them to seek the old, godly way, and walk in it.

LORD, in your mercy, hear our prayer.

Based on Jeremiah 6:16

Shelter

*Y*our unfailing love, O LORD, is as vast as the heavens; your faithfulness reaches beyond the clouds. Your righteousness is like the mighty mountains, your justice like the ocean depths. O LORD, give your protection to people and animals alike. Help them know how precious your unfailing love is. May those who suffer find shelter in the shadow of your wings. Feed them from the rich foods of your own house, letting them drink from your rivers of delight. May they know that you are the fountain of life. It is by your light that we see light, even in our darkness. Continue to show your unfailing love and mercy to those who love you; give justice to those with honest hearts.

LORD, in your mercy, hear our prayer.

Based on Psalm 36:5-12

Strength

*T*hank you that you are the sovereign God and that nothing is outside of your control. You turn evil into good and bring abundance out of deserts. Therefore, during this time of pandemic, provide those healthcare workers, grocery store associates, and others who provide essential services with strength when they are tired. Encourage those who feel insecure and anxious. Say to those with fearful hearts, "Be strong, and do not fear" for God will save you. Protect them in this time of crisis.

LORD, in your mercy, hear our prayer.

Based on Isaiah 35:1-4

Triumph

LORD, we look forward to the day when the deaf will hear and the blind will see through the gloom and darkness; when the poor will be filled with fresh joy from you, LORD; when the needy will rejoice in you, the Holy One. LORD, we pray for the day when the tyrants will be gone, the mockers will disappear, and all those who plot evil will come to an end. May those who convict the innocent by their false testimonies disappear along with those who use trickery to pervert justice and those who tell lies to destroy the innocent.

LORD, for those who live in difficult circumstances, may they be confident that in you there is hope.

Based on Isaiah 29:17-23

Understanding the times

*L*ORD, guide those who are in the midst of chaos to remember that there's a right time to do things, a right time for everything on the earth: a right time for birth and another for death; a right time to plant and another to reap; a right time to kill and another to heal; a right time to destroy and another to build; a right time to cry and another to laugh; a right time to lament and another to cheer; a right time to make love and another to abstain; a right time to embrace and another to part; a right time to search and another to count their losses; a right time to hold on and another to let go; a right time to rip out and another to mend; a right time to shut up and another to speak up; a right time to love and another to hate; a right time to wage war and another to make peace. Help us all to do all things at the proper time.

LORD, in your mercy, hear our prayer.

Based on Ecclesiastes 3:1-8

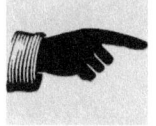

Leadership

*L*eaders carry heavy responsibilities, regardless of whether they lead countries, cities, churches, schools, businesses, or non-governmental organizations. Good leadership means success. Poor leadership can destroy the institution as well as the people working under the leader. We need to pray for our leaders at every level.

A. Government, Business, Education

Accountability

LORD, we ask that leaders always carefully think before making decisions. Be with the leaders when they make decisions, remembering they are not judging for people but for you, LORD. May they fear you, and be careful about what they do. May leaders be impartial and never take bribes. May our leaders be like you, the LORD our God, who is never unjust.

LORD, in your mercy, hear our prayer.

Based on 2 Chronicles 19:6-7

Authorities

O LORD, we urgently make requests, prayers, intercession, and thanksgiving for leaders and all those in authority, in hope that we may live peaceful and quiet lives, godly and dignified in every way. Let these requests please you, O God our Savior, for you want all people to be saved and to come to a knowledge of the truth.

LORD, in your mercy, hear our prayer.

Based on 1 Timothy 2:1-4

Choices

*L*ORD, you have given people the choice between life and death, between blessings and curses. May heaven and earth witness this choice. We pray for the nations, that their leaders would choose life so that all their people might live! Help them and help us to make this choice to love you, O LORD our God, to obey you, and to commit ourselves firmly to you, for this is the key to life. Turn the hearts of our leaders to you.

LORD, in your mercy, hear our prayer.

Based on Deuteronomy 30:19-20

Honesty

*L*ORD, we bring to you each of our political leaders, those who should represent the people to enact laws that settle their disagreements. Enable leaders to be knowledgeable about your laws so that they can proclaim your decisions, teach the people your laws and instructions, and show them how to conduct their lives. Also, help the leaders of your choice to find capable, honest people who fear God and hate bribes to come forward to help them.

LORD, in your mercy, hear our prayer.

Based on Exodus 18:19-21

Integrity

LORD, we ask for leaders to delegate responsibilities to capable, honest people who can be trusted and will not change their decisions for money. Then let those to whom responsibility is given settle the problems and issues within their domains, leaving the more difficult problems for higher levels of leadership. Then the people can have their issues successfully resolved in a timely fashion and can live in peace.

LORD, in your mercy, hear our prayer.

Based on Exodus 18:21-23

Judging rightly

O LORD, remind leaders around the world, even those who do not have your written law, that they know your law when they instinctively obey it, even without having heard or seen it. They demonstrate that your law is written in their hearts, for their own consciences and conflicting thoughts either accuse them or defend them. Cause leaders to live with the awareness that the day is coming when you, God, through Christ Jesus, will judge everyone's secret life.

LORD, in your mercy, hear our prayer.

Based on Romans 2:14-16

Justice

𝒢ive your love of justice to our leaders, O God,
and righteousness to those who are in
positions of authority. Help them judge your people
in the appropriate way. Let the poor always be treated
fairly. Remind leaders to defend the poor, to rescue the
children of the needy, and to crush oppressors. May
leaders fear you as long as the sun shines and as long as
the moon remains in the sky. May our leaders' rule be
refreshing like spring rain on freshly cut grass, like the
showers that water the land. May all the godly flourish
during their time in leadership.
May there be peace in abundance.

LORD, in your mercy, hear our prayer.

Based on Psalm 72:1-7

Prayer for peace

LORD, we pray for the peace of our city, and that all who love this city will prosper. May there be peace and justice in our streets and prosperity in our businesses. For the sake of family and friends, we ask for peace. For your sake, O LORD, help us to always seek what is best for our city, our country, and our world.

LORD, in your mercy, hear our prayer.

Based on Psalm 122:6-9

Protection

LORD, we pray that you will look on those leaders who are honest and innocent and love peace. Give them wonderful futures. LORD, save the godly; be their strength in times of trouble. LORD, help them, and save them from the wicked. Save them, and may they find shelter in you.

LORD, in your mercy, hear our prayer.

Based on Psalm 37:37, 39-40

Purity

*L*ORD, we pray for those seeking to lead us. We ask that they will be careful to live blameless lives and walk with integrity in their own homes. May they refuse to look at anything vile or vulgar. Remind them to stay clear of all who deal crookedly and to have nothing to do with dishonest people. May they reject those with devious minds and stay away from every evil. May they not tolerate people who slander their neighbors or are conceited and arrogant. Help them to search for people of integrity to be their companions. May only those who are above reproach be allowed to serve with them. Don't allow those who tell lies to serve as their advisors or liars to stay in their presence.

LORD, give us the leaders of your choice.
In your mercy, hear our prayer.

Based on Psalm 101:2-7

Repentance

*L*ORD, we pray for those leaders who think it foolish to acknowledge you. Make them aware that you could abandon them to their foolish thinking and let them do things that should never be done. Before that happens, turn their lives around so they will not become full of every kind of wickedness, sin, greed, hate, envy, murder, quarreling, deception, malicious behavior, and gossip. Prevent them from becoming backstabbers, those that hate God, who are insolent, proud, boastful, even inventing new ways of sinning. Cause them to obey your laws and not to be foolish.

Help our leaders to keep their promises and show kindness and mercy. Remind them that your justice requires those who fail to do these things to die. Even though they know this, many fail to follow your instructions. Worse yet, they encourage others to go the wrong way. Help them to repent before you pour out your trouble and suffering on those who live for themselves, who refuse to obey the truth, and instead live lives of wickedness. Show them that there will be trouble and calamity for everyone who keeps on doing what is evil.

LORD, in your mercy, hear our prayer.

Based on Romans 1:24-32, 2:8-9

Rescue from evil leaders

O LORD, it seems that many godly people have gone from the earth; it seems that scarcely any decent person is left. Instead, some leaders encourage militias to ambush people in order to commit murder. They trap each other in nets of intrigue. With both hands they are

doing evil! Officials and judges alike demand bribes. The people with influence say what they want and get it, and together they scheme to twist justice. Even the best of them is like a briar; the most honest is as dangerous as a hedge of thorns. But their judgment day is coming swiftly now. LORD, your time of punishment is here; it is a time of confusion. As for us, we look to you, LORD, for help. We wait confidently for you, God, to save us.
O God, hear us.

LORD, in your mercy, hear our prayer.

Based on Micah 7:2-4, 7

Respect for our leaders

LORD, remind all believers to place themselves under the government and its officers. We should be obedient, ready to help with every good thing they do, as long as we can do so without sinning. We must not slander anyone and must avoid quarreling. Instead, we should be gentle and show true courtesy to everyone. Help us follow your lead on these teachings so that all who trust in God can concentrate on setting an example by doing the right things, because these teachings are good and helpful for us all.

LORD, in your mercy, hear our prayer.

Based on Titus 3:1-2, 8

Self-deception

LORD, you have warned all of us, particularly our leaders, that only sorrow awaits those who say that evil is good and good is evil, that darkness is light and light is darkness, that bitter is sweet and sweet is bitter. There is only sorrow for those who are wise in their own eyes and think themselves clever. May our leaders not take bribes to let the wicked go free and then punish the innocent.

LORD, in your mercy, hear our prayer.

Based on Isaiah 5:20-23

Wisdom

LORD, may our leaders cry out for insight and understanding. Help them to seek these qualities as intently as they would search for silver or hidden treasures. Only then will they understand what it means to fear the LORD and gain knowledge from you. Thank you for granting wisdom, knowledge, and understanding to all who seek it wholeheartedly. You even give the treasure of common sense to those who are honest. Shield from evil those who live with integrity. Guard the paths of the just. For those who follow your admonitions will understand what is right, just, and fair, and you will show them the right way to go. Let wisdom enter their hearts and knowledge fill them with joy. May their wise choices prevent turmoil, and may their understanding keep them safe.

LORD, in your mercy, hear our prayer.

Based on Proverbs 2:3-11

B. Religious Leaders

Christlikeness

LORD, we pray that our pastors and church leaders whom you have chosen will please you. Put your Spirit on them and enable them to proclaim justice to the nations. Keep our leaders calm in the face of disruption and chaos, merciful to those who are weak, and an encouragment to those who are struggling. Through their ministry, may the cause of justice be victorious, and in your name may they bring hope to all the world.

LORD, in your mercy, hear our prayer.

Based on Matthew 12:18-21

Dependence

LORD, we pray that pastors will not be proud or arrogant. Help them to be dependent on you, just as a small child is dependent on his or her parent. There may be concerns for which there seem to be no answers, or the answers are still too far away to grasp. Help our pastors to be calm and quiet before you and to be content in your care and under your direction. LORD, may our pastors have hope in you, now and always.

LORD, in your mercy, hear our prayer.

Based on Psalm 131

Encouragement

O LORD, hear the cries of your servants for direction, even when they are in despair. Hear their cries and attend to their prayers. LORD, as they wait for your answer, they have been discouraged and tempted to doubt, but you offer forgiveness so they might learn to respect and trust you. Renew their faith and trust in your Word. May they long to know you more, even more than watchmen long for the dawn. May our pastors hope in you, LORD, for with you there is unfailing love. Your sovereignty is complete, and in your time, you will make known your will.

LORD, in your mercy, hear our prayer.

Based on Psalm 130

Faithfulness

LORD, we pray for the leaders of your church to faithfully teach all the truth they receive from you, the LORD All-Powerful. Guard their lips so they tell the truth and do what is just. May they live in peace and honesty, and turn many from lives of sin. Their words should preserve knowledge, and people should be able to go to them for instruction, for these leaders are your messengers, O LORD Almighty.

LORD, in your mercy, hear our prayer.

Based on Malachi 2:6-7

Godliness

*L*ORD, may the leaders of your church live blameless lives. Keep them faithful in marriage, and may their children be believers who don't have a reputation for being wild or rebellious. Enable the leaders of our faith communities to live blameless lives. May they not be arrogant or quick-tempered. Keep them from the temptation of becoming heavy drinkers. May they not become violent, or greedy for money. Rather, may they enjoy having guests in their homes and showing hospitality. May they love what is good. Help them to be self-controlled and upright. Guide them so that they live devout and disciplined lives. Keep their belief strong in the trustworthy message that was taught to them. Then our leaders will be able to encourage others with wholesome teaching and show those who oppose it where they are wrong.

LORD, in your mercy, hear our prayer.

Based on Titus 1:6-9

Good shepherds

*L*ORD, may those who act as shepherds of your people be faithful to take care of the weak, to heal the sick, and to bandage those who are injured. May they go looking for those who have wandered away or are lost. May they not rule their people harshly or violently so that the people are scattered and become easy prey for the enemy. Help the shepherds feed their people and cause them to be at peace.

LORD, in your mercy, hear our prayer.

Based on Ezekiel 34:4-5, 14

Guidance

𝒪 LORD, we pray for our pastors and church leaders as they prepare to preach and teach, that they would rely on the power of the Holy Spirit for guidance. May they speak words of wisdom. May they have the mind of Christ.

LORD, in your mercy, hear our prayer.

Based on 1 Corinthians 2:4, 6, 16

Insights

𝒪 LORD, may our pastors find joy in obeying your Word. May they find refreshment in studying and learning about you day and night. Enrich them and make them the people you want them to be so that, as they preach your word, many will come to faith in you. May our pastors be filled each day with fresh insights about you and be renewed in you each morning.

LORD, in your mercy, hear our prayer.

Based on Psalm 1

Outreach

LORD, particularly remind our leaders in the church that you have given them all authority in heaven and on earth, so they should go and make followers of all the people in the world, baptizing them in the name of the Father and the Son and the Holy Spirit. Inspire them to teach these new disciples to obey all the commands you have given. Reassure them that you are with them always, until the end of time.

LORD, in your mercy, hear our prayer.

Based on Matthew 28:18-20

Renewal

We pray for our pastors and ask that they will have all they need: rest, peace, renewed strength and guidance so that they bring honor to your name. Even when they go through dark and stressful times, be close to them so that they are not afraid. Use these trials to guide, protect, and comfort them. You are preparing blessings for them in the midst of challenges. Give them honor and blessings, goodness and unfailing love all their days as they live in your presence.

LORD, in your mercy, hear our prayer.

Based on Psalm 23

C. Congregations

Despair

LORD, we confess that there are times when we despair of finding solutions to problems in our congregation. We call on you for help. Pay attention to our prayers. LORD, if you kept track of our sins, we wouldn't survive. You offer forgiveness as we learn to respect and trust you. We are counting on you, LORD, and trusting in you and your Word to supply this need. We long to see answers to our prayers and also to know more of you. Help us to hope in you, for you are the source of unfailing love. Your cup of blessing overflows, and you will fulfill our petitions at the right times. Cleanse us from our sins so that we may be prepared for your answer.

LORD, in your mercy, hear our prayer.

Based on Psalm 130

Focus

O God, you are our refuge and strength, always present to help us. Keep us focused on you, even when our foundations are shaken and our expectations crumble before our eyes. Though the world's chaos rages, let your presence among us refresh us, secure us, and supply our needs. Though there are turmoil and trouble all around us, we are secure in your fortress. Your power and work continually amaze us. Our focus can wander, so help us to be still and know that you are God: be still and know you; be still; be. In this way we will honor you in our church, our city, our nation, and our world. You are here among us, and we rejoice in that!

LORD, in your mercy, hear our prayer.

Based on Psalm 46

Guidance

O LORD, keep our congregation true to you. May we not be tempted to give up on you and seek our own way. Help those who may be weak in faith not to give up on you. Instead, may we all find encouragement, joy, and guidance as we obey your Word and study it regularly.
Help us to grow like trees—with our roots being fed and nourished by the waters of Scripture. May our faith be fruitful and vibrant as we witness your faithfulness.
Guide us and protect us from discouragement.

LORD, in your mercy, hear our prayer.

Based on Psalm 1

Provision

*L*ORD, remind us that you are our Shepherd and you give us all that we need. Help us to rest in the abundant provision you've made for us to be at peace, especially in times of uncertainty and change. Continue to renew our fellowship together, lead us into making good plans and decisions so that we bring honor to your name. Even when we are confronted with difficulties, opposition, and apparent failure, help us not to be afraid but to remember that you are close at hand and always among us. May the church leadership and your Word be protecting us from evil and providing the comfort we need. You are preparing us for a wonderful blessing. Help us to be ready and open to the direction of your Spirit. Then we will overflow with blessings, and your goodness and unfailing love will pursue us as a congregation for years to come as we worship together as your people.

LORD, in your mercy, hear our prayer.

Based on Psalm 23

Trust

LORD, forgive us for our pride and haughtiness in our expectations for our churches. At times we feel anxious and concern ourselves with issues that don't belong to us, trying to solve issues like global politics, wars, the migrant and opioid crises that are too complex and too serious for us to truly understand. We ask that you calm and quiet our hearts so that we can rest and be at peace with you and ourselves. May we put our hope in you, now and always.

LORD, in your mercy, hear our prayer.

Based on Psalm 131

D. Pastoral Search Team

It often takes a long time and much searching to replace a pastor who is loved and appreciated. The search team needs support and prayers. These prayers, based on the Psalms, may be helpful for the congregation and the team to pray.

Direction

Thank you for not holding our faults and weaknesses against us. Otherwise, there would be no hope at all. You generously forgive; thus, we learn forgiveness.

We are counting on you, O LORD, expecting you to answer our prayers. We are putting our hope in you and the promises in your word. We've come to know more of you in this process and long to know you more. We hope in you, O LORD, for your love is unfailing, and your salvation overflows. You alone will answer our prayers for a pastor to lead us along the paths where you want us to go.

LORD, in your mercy, hear our prayer.

Based on Psalm 130

Guidance

O LORD, for those on our pastoral search team, may they be guided in their task and be protected from the "advice" from the enemy to give up. Don't let them be discouraged by the negative responses they receive.

Help them to delight in you and in the work they have undertaken. As they listen and reflect on the choices before them, may they be strengthened, enlightened, cautioned and directed. Day and night, keep them focused on you and be renewed and filled each day by the power of your Spirit within them. Watch over their paths and lead them to the pastor of your choice.

LORD, in your mercy, hear our prayer.

Based on Psalm 1

Patience

L ORD, help us all to wait quietly before you, for you are the source of our success. Keep us abiding in you as our stability and provision, a safe place that will never be shaken.

People become impatient and want results that the search team cannot yet provide. People may think the team is ineffective or unable to carry out their directive. Others may speak positively but fail to pray for the team.

Let us wait quietly before you, O God, for our hope is in you. You are the only one we can depend on, the only safe place that will never be shaken. Only you can give us success. You are our refuge.

May we trust in you at all times, pouring out our hearts to you—for you are our refuge. Answer our prayers, O God, in your time because of your unfailing love.

LORD, in your mercy, hear our prayer.

Based on Psalm 62

Protection

Thank you, LORD, for being a refuge and strength to the pastoral search team. You have been with them throughout this process. So, when troubles or disappointments or criticisms come, help them not to fear but to be reminded of the protection and joy they have and will continue to experience as they walk daily with you, for you are the great GOD that cannot be destroyed. You will protect your people from the beginning to the end, no matter how chaotic, crazy, or out-of-control things become. LORD, be our Captain, the one who leads us as we trust in you.

Help the pastoral search team to be still and know that you are God. May you be honored throughout this church, this nation, and the world. You are here among us and you are our fortress.

LORD, in your mercy, hear our prayer.

Based on Psalm 46

Provision

LORD, we pray that the pastoral search team will have all the resources and information they need. Keep them at peace and resting in you. Guide them in the right paths so they bring honor to your name. The dark valley of discouragement can cause distress and make them fear that they are not doing enough, but we ask for your presence to keep them from those concerns, and to protect and comfort them. Remind them of the reward you are preparing for them when they complete this important task. Pour your anointing oil over their heads to drive away doubts. May their lives overflow with blessings, for surely your goodness and unfailing love will pursue them all the days of their lives as they live out your calling.

LORD, in your mercy, hear our prayer.

Based on Psalm 23

Trust

LORD, help us to acknowledge our inadequacies and any pride or haughtiness that may have come with this position. We don't want to concern ourselves with matters that are too great or too awesome to grasp. Instead, help us to calm and quiet ourselves, like a weaned child who no longer cries for its mother's milk. Yes, may we be satisfied and content in you and put our hope in you, LORD, now and always.

LORD, in your mercy, hear our prayer.

Based on Psalm 131

Migrant, Persecuted and Refugee Communities

Many people are crossing the Mediterranean Sea or sending children through war-torn countries, living for ten to twenty years in squalid refugee camps, or camping out on the border of the United States. Why? They are fleeing situations in their home countries that are intolerable. They face persecution because of religious or political convictions, insecurity, or hopeless poverty. To make moves requiring such danger indicate the desperation the individual or family faces. Some have arrived illegally in a country and live in fear. There are thousands more who don't leave their homes but continue to suffer and need our prayers.

Comfort

O God, you are compassionate and the God who gives comfort. Please comfort each person whatever their troubles so that they can experience your love and care, and find true peace. Then when they meet others in similar circumstances, they will be able to pass on your comfort to them. We know you suffered so much for us; you understand how we feel, and we get so much comfort from you.

LORD, in your mercy, may all who suffer find comfort in you.

Based on 2 Corinthians 1:3-5

Discouragement

*L*ORD, we remember those who are suffering because they trust in you. They may feel like a piece of broken pottery, faded from memory as if they were dead. They have heard many insults. Terror is all around them. Their enemies scheme together against them and plot to kill them. LORD, may your people trust you. May they continue to know and say, "You are my God."

Their lives are in your hands. Rescue them from their

enemies and from those who are seeking them. Show your kindness to your servants. Save them because of your love. LORD, we call to you on their behalf, so do not let them be disgraced.

LORD, in your mercy, hear our prayer.

Based on Psalm 31:12-17

Distress

We pray for those with psychological, emotional, or physical problems to find hope and be able to discover a way out of their situations. May the poor hear the Good News, the proclamation that captives will be released, that the blind will see, that the oppressed will be set free, and that the time of the LORD's favor has come.

LORD, in your mercy, hear our prayer.

Based on Luke 4:18-19a

Endurance

O LORD, when people are undergoing difficult times, help them to remember that the word of God cannot be

bound. Help them to be willing to endure anything if it will bring salvation and eternal glory in Christ Jesus to those whom God has chosen.
Remind them of this trustworthy saying:
If they die with you, they will also live with you.
If they endure hardship, they will reign with you.
If they deny you, you will deny them.
If they are unfaithful, you remain faithful,
for you cannot deny yourself.

LORD, in your mercy, hear our prayer.

Based on 2 Timothy 2:9-13

Endurance

When people have troubles all around them, O LORD, protect them from being crushed and broken. When they are frustrated and have no idea what to do, encourage them so they will not give up and quit. When they are persecuted, never abandon them. When they get knocked down, help them get up again and keep going, so that the life of Jesus may also be seen in them.

LORD, in your mercy, hear our prayer.

Based on 2 Corinthians 4:8-10

Generosity

O LORD, remind us that a farmer who plants only a few seeds will get a small harvest, but the one who plants generously will get a generous crop. Each person must decide how much to give to those in need. And we shouldn't give reluctantly or in response to pressure, for you "love a person who gives cheerfully." And God, we trust you will generously provide all we need. Then we will always have everything we need and plenty left over to share with others. As the Scriptures say, "They share freely and give generously to the poor. Their good deeds will be remembered forever."

Help us to be generous in our giving to those in need.

LORD, in your mercy, hear our prayer.

Based on 2 Corinthians 9:6-9

Homelessness

*F*or all those who have run from their homes because of threats, suffering, and fear, may they find hope in God, for you want them to be loved and live in peace without fear. We know that you love all the peoples of the world. You are Love. And as we live in you, our love grows more mature and confident. So, may those who come to know and love you not be afraid but seek life with confidence. We know that fear cannot exist where there is love. Instead, love gets rid of fear. May each fearful person find perfect love and freedom from fear in your home.

LORD, in your mercy, hear our prayer.

Based on 1 John 4:16b-18

Hope

*L*ORD, surely you have seen and taken note of your people's trouble and grief and placed them under your control. These people who are in trouble are looking to you for guidance. You are the One who helps the needy. Break the power of the wicked and evil people who hurt others. Punish them for the evil they do. LORD, you are King forever and ever. Remove godless nations from the earth. LORD, you know the hopes of the helpless. Hear their cries and comfort them. Protect the orphans and put an end to their suffering so that they will no longer need to be afraid because of evil people.

LORD, in your mercy, hear our prayer.

Based on Psalm 10:14-18

Justice

*M*ay those who rejoice at the calamity of the innocent be humiliated and embarrassed. May those who promote themselves at the expense of the godly be covered with shame and disgrace. LORD, give great joy to those who have stood with the righteous in their defense. Let them continually say, "Great is the LORD who enjoys helping his servant." Then may your people tell everyone of your justice and goodness and praise you all day long.

LORD, in your mercy, hear our prayer.

Based on Psalm 35:26-28

Justice for persecutors

O LORD, hear the believers as they cry out, "How long must we wait? When will you bring to justice those who persecute us?" These arrogant people who hate your instructions have dug deep pits to trap your people. Since all your commands are trustworthy, protect your people from those who persecute them with lies or hunt them down without cause. Their enemies have almost wiped them from the face of the earth, but help your people never to abandon the guidance found in your

Word. In your unfailing love, give the persecuted new life, and cause those who persecute them to obey your laws.

LORD, in your mercy, hear our prayer.

Based on Psalm 119:84-88

Love

Father, we know what real love is because Jesus laid down his life for us. So, we also ought to give up our lives for our brothers and sisters. Remind us that if someone has enough money to live well and sees a brother or sister in need, but shows no compassion—God's love cannot abide in that person! Help us not merely to say that we love each other; let us show the truth by what we do. Guide our actions to show that we belong to the truth, so we will be confident when we stand before you, O God.

LORD, in your mercy, hear our prayer.

Based on 1 John 3:16-19

Love for enemies

*L*ORD, help our brothers and sisters facing persecution to follow your command to love their enemies and to pray for those who persecute them. Remind them that by doing so, they will be acting as true children of their Father in heaven. For you make the sun rise on both the evil and the good, and you send rain on the just and on the unjust, too. Also remind them that they are to be perfect, even as their Father in heaven is perfect.

LORD, in your mercy, hear our prayer.

Based on Matthew 5:44-45, 48

Loving the stranger

*L*ORD, our God, you are the God of all gods and LORD of all lords. You are the great God, the strong and wonderful God. You show no partiality and cannot be bribed into doing evil. Give our leaders hearts that reflect yours to ensure that the powerless receive the help they need. Show us how to love all of those living among us by giving them food and clothing, for we, or our ancestors, were once strangers and needed help.

LORD, in your mercy, hear our prayer.

Based on Deuteronomy 10:17-19

Mistreatment

*L*ORD, you have firmly told us we must not mistreat or oppress people in any way, especially those who are not like us. We are to remember that we or our ancestors were once "the newcomers, the different ones." Help us not to exploit widows or orphans because if we do and they cry out to you, then you will certainly hear their cries and punish us.

LORD, in your mercy, hear our prayer.

Based on Exodus 22:21-23

Opposition

*L*ORD, we pray for those who persecute your followers, arresting both men and women and throwing them in prison, even hounding some to death. Many persecutors also have the backing of the authorities to bring Christians from their homes or even airports to be punished. Remind your children that Jesus the Nazarene is the One who they are really opposing. And we pray that, like Saul, you will pour out your special favor on these persecutors and change their hearts. May those who are now persecutors repent and work harder to further your kingdom than any of the Christians they persecuted; as you, God, work through them by your grace.

LORD, in your mercy, hear our prayer.

Based on Acts 22:4-5, 8 and 1 Corinthians 15:10

Peace and safety

 ℒORD, we pray for people who find themselves wandering in unknown and sometimes hostile lands. They can find no safe place to stay. They are hungry and thirsty, and they are discouraged. In their misery, they cry out to you, LORD. Save them from their troubles. Lead them on a straight road to a place where they can live in peace and safety. Satisfy the thirsty and fill up the hungry with good things. Then may they give thanks to you, LORD, for your love and for the miracles you do for them.

LORD, in your mercy, hear our prayer.

Based on Psalm 107:4-9

Persecution

 ℒORD, your people are being arrested and treated cruelly. Sometimes they are put in jail and must appear before judges for being your followers. Give them the courage and opportunity to tell these leaders about you. Help them not to worry about how to answer the charges against them. Give them the right words and the wisdom to say things that none of their opponents will be able to stand against or prove wrong!

LORD, in your mercy, hear our prayer.

Based on Luke 21:12-15

Protection

Our help comes from you, LORD, who made heaven and earth! Don't let suffering people stumble, watch over them without closing your eyes. Be the guardian who watches over your people without ever falling asleep. LORD, watch over your precious ones! Stand beside them as a protective shade, so the sun will not beat down on them during the day nor the moon at night. LORD, guard them from every evil and protect their lives. Keep watch over them as they come and go, both now and forever.

LORD, in your mercy, hear our prayer.

Based on Psalm 121:2-8

Refuge

O LORD, turn to the refugees fleeing to safety, and have pity on them, for they are lonely and in deep distress. Feel their pain and see their trouble. Forgive all their sins. See how many enemies they have and how they are hated with vicious anger!

Protect the refugees! Rescue their lives from their enemies! Do not let them be disgraced, for in you they take refuge. May integrity and honesty protect them as they put their hope in you, O God. Ransom them from all their troubles.

LORD, in your mercy, hear our prayer.

Based on Psalm 25:16-22

Refugees

O loving and compassionate God, women and children are left like homeless birds at the borders of our land. "Help us," they cry. They ask us to help defend them from their enemies and protect them from relentless attacks. They beg not to be betrayed now that they have managed to escape from danger. They ask to stay hidden from their enemies until the terror has passed, when their oppressors and their enemies have disappeared.

LORD, establish in our land those who will rule with mercy and truth, eager to do what is just, and doing what is right.

LORD, in your mercy, hear our prayer.

Based on Isaiah 16:2-5

Repentance

O LORD, pour out your fury on the nations that refuse to acknowledge you— on kingdoms that do not call upon your name. For they have devoured your people, destroying homes and lands. But when they call out to you in repentance, do not hold them guilty for their sins! Reach out quickly with your compassion and meet their needs when they are on the brink of despair. Help them, O God of our salvation! Help them turn to you for the glory of your name. Save them and forgive their sins for the honor of your name.

LORD, in your mercy, hear our prayer.

Based on Psalm 79:6-9

Rescue

LORD, we pray that you will rescue the needy people when they cry to you; save the oppressed people when no one else will help them. Have pity on the poor and needy and save their lives. Rescue them from oppression and from violence, for their lives are precious to you.

LORD, in your mercy, hear our prayer.

Based on Psalm 72:12-14

Restoration

O LORD, come to your people who have had to leave their homelands. Do all the good things you have promised. Bring them back to their own homes again. For you know you have good plans for them. They are plans for good and not for disaster. You have plans to give your people a hope and a good future. In those days when they pray, listen. If they look for you wholeheartedly, may they find you. Show yourself to them, O LORD. Bring them back from their exile and restore their fortunes. Gather them out of the nations where they have run and bring them home again to their own land.

LORD, in your mercy, hear our prayer.

Based on Jeremiah 29:10-14

Retribution

*L*ORD, when the wicked set traps for the godly, they defiantly snarl at the weak and oppressed. But LORD, you just laugh at the wicked, for you see their day of judgment coming. The wicked plan their scams and schemes to take advantage of the poor and the oppressed, to destroy those who do right. We pray that the plans of the wicked will do no damage, and their instruments of destruction will be broken.

LORD, in your mercy, hear our prayer.

Based on Psalm 37:12-15

Revenge

*H*elp each person to do his or her part to live in peace with everyone, as much as possible. Help people to never take revenge themselves but leave that to you, O God. For you have said, "I will take vengeance; I will repay those who deserve it." Instead, cause people to do what the Scriptures say. If your enemies are hungry, feed them. If they are thirsty, give them a drink, and they will be surprised with goodness. Don't let evil get the best of them but conquer evil by doing good.

LORD, in your mercy, hear our prayer.

Based on Romans 12:18-21

Safety

O LORD, we have come to ask you to protect your servants; don't let them be disgraced. Save them because you do what is right. Listen to them; rescue them quickly. Be their rock of protection, a fortress where they will be safe. You are their rock and their fortress. For the honor of your name, lead and guide them out of whatever danger they are in. Pull them from the traps their enemies set for them, for you alone are their protection. We entrust their spirits into your hand. Rescue them, LORD, for you are a faithful God.

LORD, in your mercy, hear our prayer.

Based on Psalm 31:1-5

Security

O LORD, may your people not lose sight of sound wisdom and discretion but hang on to them, for your wisdom will keep their souls alive and well. Help your children to see that wisdom and discernment are like jewels on a necklace. These principles keep them safe on their way, so their feet will not stumble. Let them know they can go to bed without fear, lie down, and sleep soundly. Assure them that they need not panic in a sudden disaster or when destruction comes to the wicked, for you, LORD, are their security. Keep them from being caught in traps of fear or anxiety.

LORD, in your mercy, hear our prayer.

Based on Proverbs 3:21-26

Sovereignty

Let everyone fear you, LORD. Cause people to stand in awe of you. For when you spoke, the world began! You gave the order, and there it stood. LORD, shatter the plans of those bringing chaos and strife, and thwart all their schemes. May your people know that your plans stand firm forever; your intentions and purposes can never be shaken.

LORD, in your mercy, hear our prayer.

Based on Psalm 33:8-11

Standing firm

LORD, many persecute and trouble your people, so help your children not to swerve from your way. Seeing traitors makes us sick at heart because they care nothing for your word nor do they believe your promises.

See how your servants love your commandments, LORD. Give them back their lives because of your unfailing love. The very essence of your word is truth, and all your righteous regulations will stand forever. So, when powerful people harass your servants without any reason, stand with your people so their hearts tremble only at your word.

LORD, in your mercy, hear our prayer.

Based on Psalm 119:157-161

Support

Thank you, LORD, for the example of those saints who stood their ground in the face of hardship and pain. We pray for those who are publicly insulted and mistreated, and we pray for those who stand side by side with those who are so treated. We remember those in prison and pray that even those whose property is confiscated will be joyful because they remember they have better and more permanent possessions. Help them not to lose their confidence but trust that their faith will be richly rewarded. Help them to endure so that when they have done your will, they will receive what you have promised.

LORD, in your mercy, hear our prayer.

Based on Hebrews 10:32-36

Victory over our enemies

*L*ORD, blow your breath on your enemies, so the sea will cover them. Let them sink like lead in the raging water. Who is like you among the gods, O LORD—glorious because of your holiness, awesome in splendor, performing miracles? Raise your right hand, and let the earth swallow your enemies. With your unfailing love, lead to safety the people you have redeemed. By your might, guide them to your sacred home.

LORD, in your mercy, hear our prayer.

Based on Exodus 15:10-13

Natural Disasters

In the past few years we have had a record number of fires, floods, hurricanes and damaging tornadoes. Africa has also suffered with plagues of locust, sometimes more than once in a year. The people that suffer from these various disasters need our prayers.

Care for our world

*L*ORD, we recognize that you made human beings in your own image and likeness and gave us the responsibility to rule over the fish in the sea, the birds in the sky, the tame animals, the wild animals, and even the small, crawling animals. You told us to fill the earth and be in charge. We are to rule over everything that moves on the earth. We have not taken this charge seriously. We have greedily used the resources of this world, and we have not cared for the life and welfare of this planet of ours. Forgive us, LORD, for our selfishness and disobedience.

LORD, in your mercy, forgive.

Based on Genesis 1:27-30

Deliverance

*L*ORD, we ask that you deliver your people from all deadly peril, and we know that you are able to deliver us. We have set our hope on you that you will continue to deliver us all as we offer up our prayers. Then may we all give thanks for the gracious favor granted in answer to our prayers.

LORD, in your mercy, hear our prayer.

Based on 2 Corinthians 1:10-11

Drought

*L*ORD, the seeds shrivel in the soil; our storehouses are empty, and barns are torn down, for the grain has dried up. The animals groan and wander aimlessly looking for pasture. LORD, we cry to you, for the heat has devoured the pastures, even in the wilderness. The drought has burned up all the trees of the field, and even the animals pant for you, for the brooks and streams have dried up, and fire has devoured the pastures.

LORD, in your mercy, hear our prayer.

Based on Joel 1:17-20

Earthquakes

O God, you are our protection and our strength. We beg for your help in these times of trouble. Help us and all your people not to be afraid even when the earth shakes or the mountains fall into the sea, even if the oceans churn and foam. Nations tremble and kingdoms shake. God, you shout and the earth crumbles. Help us all to remember that the LORD All-Powerful is with us, for you, O God, are our defender.

LORD, in your mercy, hear our prayer.

Based on Psalm 46:1-3, 6-7

Famine

*L*ORD, watch over those who fear you and rely on your unfailing love. Rescue them from death and keep them alive in this time of famine. Cause them to put their hope in you, LORD, for you are their help and shield. Cause their hearts to rejoice in you and to trust in your holy name. Let your unfailing love surround them, LORD, and let their hope be in you alone.

LORD, in your mercy, hear our prayer.

Based on Psalm 33:18-22

Floods

*W*hen the earth quakes and its people live in turmoil, LORD, keep their foundations firm. Save the people in this disaster area, O God, for the floodwaters are up to their necks. Deeper and deeper they sink into the mire; they can't find footholds to stand on. They are in deep water, and the floods overwhelm them. They are exhausted from crying for help; their throats are parched and dry. Their eyes are swollen with weeping, waiting for you, God, to help them. Rescue them from the mud; don't let them sink any deeper. Pull them out of these deep waters.

LORD, in your mercy, hear our prayer.

Based on Psalm 69:1-3, 14-15

Food supplies

O LORD, after the destruction of the locusts, will you make up for all that the swarming locusts have eaten? Will you make up for the creeping locust, the stripping locust, and the gnawing locust—that great army you allowed to invade the land? Please provide so that people have enough to eat and be satisfied. We will praise the name of the LORD our God. Please deal kindly with us. May we, your people, never be put to shame. Live among us always. Cause us to remember that you are God, and there is no other.

LORD, in your mercy, hear our prayer.

Based on Joel 2:25-27

Loss of control

*L*ORD, the earth shakes and shivers! It seems that everything is rocking back and forth, out of control. Scorching heat and fiery flames are spewing from the mountains. The earth and all its people are terrified by this display of sheer power. Fiery flames light up the sky as the thunder rolls. You have shaken the earth to its very foundations.

Reach down and lift your people out of this chaos. Rescue them from the elements that seek to destroy them. The forces are too powerful for any of us. Disaster has struck, but you can defend, free, and rescue people because you love them. God, come to their aid.

LORD, in your mercy, hear our prayer.

Based on 2 Samuel 22:8, 11, 16-20

Plagues of locust

LORD, this plague of locusts will be talked about for generations. What the gnawing locust left behind, the swarming locust ate. What the swarming locust left, the creeping locust ate; and what the creeping locust left, the stripping locust ate. It is as though a nation has invaded the land. They are mighty and without number. Their teeth are like those of a lion and they have fangs like a lioness. The vines are wasted. The trees are in splinters. Everything is stripped bare, and there are no leaves left on the branches. We wail and mourn, for there will be no food or drink after this invasion. LORD, what will we do now? Come to our aid.

LORD, in your mercy, hear our prayer.

Based on Joel 1:2-4, 6-7

Rebelliousness

LORD, forgive our stubborn and rebellious hearts. Forgive all of us who have turned away and abandoned you. There are many times we do not say from the heart, "Let us live in awe of the LORD our God, for he gives us rain each spring and fall, assuring us of a harvest when the time is right." Wickedness has deprived the land of these wonderful blessings. Sin has robbed your people of all these good things.

O LORD, in your great mercy, forgive.

Based on Jeremiah 5:23-25

Relief from drought

LORD, we cry out to you because the fields are ruined and the land mourns. The grain is ruined and all resources have dried up because there is no rain. Even the trees in the fields have dried up. Indeed, rejoicing dries up in our communities. We cry out to you, O God, to relieve our suffering and send rain.

LORD, in your mercy, hear our prayer.

Based on Joel 1:10, 12

Rescue

*O*cean waves surround your people, O LORD; they are about to be swallowed by flood waters. It seems as though death is the only option; there is no escape. The victims of this flooding are in terrible trouble, so when they call out to you, hear them, hear me, and answer our prayers so that they can be rescued.

LORD, in your mercy, hear our prayer.

Based on 2 Samuel 22:5-7

Tornadoes and hurricanes

*O*ur LORD and our God, you are our mighty rock, fortress, and protector when fires, storms, tornadoes, or hurricanes come. Be the place where we can find safety. You are a shield, a powerful weapon, and a place of shelter. Rescue your people and keep them from harm.

I praise you, our LORD! When those in need pray to you, rescue them.

LORD, in your mercy, hear our prayer.

Based on 2 Samuel 22:2-4

Racism and Prejudice

In recent days, the subject of racism has made many headlines. If we are honest with ourselves, we often shy away from "the other", those who are not like like "us". God asks us to love our neighbors, regardless of who they are or what their background is. We are even asked to love our enemies and do good to those who hate us. These prayers may help direct our thoughts in a more godly direction.

Children of light

*L*ORD, help us not to live in the old ways where minds are full of darkness, wandering far from the life you give. Convict those who have closed their minds and hardened their hearts against you and have no sense of shame. May your Spirit renew their thoughts and attitudes, giving them a new nature that is righteous and holy. May they tell the truth to their neighbors and overcome the anger that controls them, for anger gives an opportunity for evil to enter our lives. May they no longer use foul or abusive language. Let everything they say be good and helpful and an encouragement to those who hear. May they get rid of all bitterness, rage, anger, harsh words, and slander, as well as all types of evil behavior. Instead, may we be kind to each other, tenderhearted, forgiving one another, just as God through Christ has forgiven us.

LORD, in your mercy, hear our prayer.

Based on Ephesians 4:17-32

Christ's example

*L*ORD, you have called us to do good, even if it means that we suffer for it. We are to follow Christ's example, but we fail all too often. He never sinned or deceived anyone, but we deceive ourselves as well as others by the way our thoughts and attitudes do not match what we say. Christ didn't retaliate when he was insulted or threaten to get revenge, but we focus on retaliation and revenge for even the smallest inconveniences. Christ left his fate in your hands because you, O God, always judge fairly. We confess that we have wandered away from you. Turn us back to you, the Shepherd and Guardian of our souls.

LORD, in your mercy, hear our prayer.

Based on 1 Peter 2:22-23, 25

Confession

O LORD, we confess that we have sinned against you and our fellow humans. You expected to find justice, but instead you found oppression. You expected to find righteousness, but instead you have heard and still hear cries of violence. LORD, we have failed you. Cause us to repent and turn and treat all of our brothers and sisters with respect and justice.

LORD, in your mercy, hear our prayer.

Based on Isaiah 5:7

Dark paths

LORD, we need you to save us from evil people who twist their words and turn from the right way to walk down dark paths. Some people seem to take pleasure in doing what is wrong and enjoy the twisted ways of evil. Their actions are crooked and their ways are wrong. But you, LORD, can turn evil people into those who do what is right and just and fair. Help them find the right way to go by giving them wisdom and knowledge that will replace their hate with joy. Help us to make wise choices and give us understanding as we remember that you watch over us and can keep us safe.

LORD, in your mercy, hear our prayer.

Based on Proverbs 2:9-15

Freedom from oppression

LORD, I ask that you free your people from the oppression under which they live. Rescue them from the hands of those who see them as inferior because they are different by the color of their skin, a disability, or intellectual acuity. Redeem your people with your power and great acts of judgment. Claim them as your own people, LORD, and be their God. May they know that you have promised to free them and bring them out of their bondage.

LORD, in your mercy, hear our prayer.

Based on Exodus 6:6-7

Living in the light

LORD, some of us think we are living "in the light" but hate others because they are different from us. Those differences may be economic, racial, social, or sexual. You tell us that if we hate our fellow believer, then we are still in darkness. Cause us to live in the light, love our fellow believers, and not do anything to cause others to stumble. LORD, help those who hate others to recognize they are still living and walking in darkness, for they don't know the right way to go, having been blinded by the darkness in their hearts.

LORD, in your mercy, hear our prayer.

Based on 1 John 2:9-11

New hearts

*L*ORD, I ask that you give us new hearts and new spirits that reflect yours. Take out our stony, stubborn, prejudiced attitudes toward those who are unlike us in some way. Give us tender, responsive, loving hearts to look for you in each one we meet. Put your Spirit within us so that we will follow your way of love and compassion.

LORD, in your mercy, hear our prayer.

Based on Ezekiel 36:26-27

One body in Christ

*L*ORD, you have brought all your children, Jews and Gentiles of all nations, ethnic groups, languages, and health conditions into your body, the church. You tell us we are no longer strangers or foreigners or "the other." We are all citizens and members of your family. Together we make up your house, and the cornerstone of that house is Jesus Christ. You have carefully brought us together and made us all part of this dwelling where you live by your Spirit. Help us to live up to your intention.

LORD, in your mercy, hear our prayer.

Based on Ephesians 2:19-22

Self-deceit

LORD, we confess that the human heart is the most deceitful of all things and desperately wicked. We cannot truly know how bad it is, but LORD, you search all hearts and examine even our secret motives. Alert us to times when we think of ourselves as superior or of someone else as inferior, for these thoughts are false. Cleanse our minds and attitudes so that when you judge us, our actions and our motives will not disappoint you. Keep us aware that you will judge according to what our actions deserve.

LORD, in your mercy, hear our prayer.

Based on Jeremiah 17:9-10

Sexual Abuse and Pornography

Many people are being lured into pornography as sex becomes the "god" of our age. Women and children are abused and trafficked to satisfy these lusts. It is a dark world that Christians do not want to know about, but it is too terrible for us to ignore. Let us pray for those who suffer and for those who promote and cause this suffering.

Children

We cry out to you, LORD, on behalf of children who are being sexually abused and trafficked. When people are tempted to abuse or traffic others, may they remember that only sorrow awaits them. Convict them of the evil of their thoughts and plans. Jesus said it would be better to be thrown into the sea with a millstone hung around the neck than to cause a child to fall into sin. Protect these children who are or have been affected by sexual abuse.

LORD, in your mercy, hear our prayer.

Based on Luke 17:1-2

Guarding one's eyes

LORD, we ask that those who are tempted to seek out pornography or other enticements will learn to control their sexual urges and guard their hearts and eyes from lust. Don't let their passions get out of hand. May they see others as people created in your image and precious to you, rather than as an object to be viewed for their own sexual gratification. Help them to avoid places and activities that would tempt them. Deliver them from situations where seduction would surely lead them to destruction.

LORD, in your mercy, hear our prayer.

Based on Proverbs 7:25

Healing

𝒪 LORD, you are a God of compassion and mercy! You are slow to become angry and full of unfailing love and faithfulness. You lavish your unfailing love on a thousand generations, forgiving iniquity, rebellion, and sin. We cry out to you today on behalf of all people who have been betrayed and deceived by wicked people.

For the wicked who traffic women and children to those who are twisted and caught up in sexual sin, we ask that you not excuse them, for they are guilty. Punish them for the harm they have done.

For those who have experienced such abuse, we ask that they may find you to be the great Healer who is able to bring wholeness into their broken lives. Rescue them, LORD, and bring them to a place of safety where they can find hope and restoration.

LORD, in your mercy, hear our prayer.

Based on Exodus 34:6-7

Obsession with sex

*L*ORD, we confess that as a nation and as a world, we have become obsessed with sex and have too often allowed temptations to lure us into sinful thoughts and actions. You have commanded us to run from sexual sin. We have forgotten or tried to ignore the fact that sexual sin affects the body more than any other sin because it is a sin against ourselves! Remind us that our bodies are the temple of the Holy Spirit, who lives in us and are given to us by God! We do not belong to ourselves, for you bought us with the price of Jesus' death on the cross. LORD, forgive us and cause us to always honor you with our bodies.

LORD, in your mercy, hear our prayer.

Based on 1 Corinthians 6:18-20

Parents

*L*ORD, we cry out to you for parents trying to raise their children in these challenging and often dangerous times. Guide parents as they teach their children in wise ways about the dangers of the Internet, social media, and sexual predators. May they prepare their children at home, as they travel, when they go to bed, and when they get up, so that when children venture into less safe spaces, they will be alert and able to confidently ward off danger. Then, LORD, may the children flourish and prosper.

LORD, in your mercy, hear our prayer.

Based on Deuteronomy 22:19-20

Pornography

LORD, you have told us that we are not to associate with anyone who claims to be a believer yet indulges in sexual sin, is greedy, abusive, a drunkard, or cheats people. You told us not to even eat with such people. While it isn't our responsibility to judge people outside the community of faith, it certainly is our responsibility to judge those believers who are sinning. We leave judgment of those outside the church to you, O God; but as the Scriptures say, "You must remove the evil person from among you." May we act in accordance with your commands that they may see the error of their ways, repent and be restored.

LORD, in your mercy, hear our prayer.

Based on 1 Corinthians 5:11-13

Predators

*L*ORD, we bring to you those who brag about themselves with empty, foolish boasting. Those who have twisted sexual desires lure others into sin, even those who have barely escaped from a lifestyle of deception. These boastful ones think they are free, but they end up as the slaves of sin and corruption, for we know we are slaves to whatever controls us. LORD, we pray for those who escape this sinful and corrupt world by coming to faith in our LORD and Savior Jesus Christ. Help them to get untangled and freed from sin, or they will be worse off than they were before. Lord have mercy on them so they come to a knowledge of the truth and be truly set free.

LORD, in your mercy, hear our prayer.

Based on 2 Peter 2:18-20

Punishment

*L*ORD, you know how to rescue godly people from the difficulties that they face. You also know how to punish the wicked as they wait for the final judgment. We pray that you will appropriately punish those who follow their own twisted sexual desires and despise authority.

LORD, in your mercy, hear our prayer.

Based on 2 Peter 2:9-10

Sexual abuse

*L*ORD, as you know all too well, today's society is marked by sexual abuse within families. You have given us instructions about how we should behave toward each other. As Jesus' followers we should be careful to obey your rules and regulations so that we can find life through them as you promised.

[6]"You must never have sexual relations with a close relative, for I am the LORD. [7]Do not violate your father by having sexual relations with you mother. [9]Do not have sexual relations with your sister or half-sister. [10]Do not have sexual relations with your daughter or granddaughter. [17]Do not have sexual relations with a woman and her daughter or her granddaughter. They are close relatives, and this would be a wicked act."

Keep us on guard against temptation and self-deceit. Protect our family relationships so that we do not offend you or each other.

LORD, in your mercy, hear our prayer.

Based on Leviticus 18:6-7, 9-10, 17

Sinful desires

LORD, we pray for those who have given in to their sinful natures and continue to do the opposite of what the Holy Spirit wants them to do. They have followed their own sinful desires, and the results are clear: sexual immorality, impurity, lustful pleasures, idolatry, sorcery, hostility, quarreling, jealousy, outbursts of anger, selfish ambition, dissension, division, envy, drunkenness, wild parties, and other sins like these. Convict them of their self-deceit and sin because you have told us that anyone living that sort of life will not inherit the Kingdom of God.

LORD, in your mercy, hear our prayer.

Based on Galatians 5:16-21

Violence, Terrorism, and War

Civil war, ethnocide, and genocide are words we hear all too often these days. Likewise, we hear of gender violence, torture, human trafficking, and other behaviors that most regard as simply evil. Wherever families are being torn apart, destroyed, or people being treated as less than human, our prayers need to be there. We should not let evil go unanswered.

Aggression

Loving LORD, would you diligently guard people who are in the middle of conflicts? Hide them in the shelter of your wings. Protect them from those who would attack them and from those who surround these people with murderous intent. We see evidence that evil people are without pity. You hear their boasting! These ungodly people track down people, surround them, and seek to destroy them. They act like hungry lions that are eager to tear innocent people into pieces. Arise, O LORD! Stand against the wicked and bring them to their knees in repentance. Rescue innocent people from the wicked, and, if you must, use your weapons against them. Save your people by your mighty hand. Save them from those whose only concern is earthly gain. Satisfy the hunger of those you treasure. May their children have plenty of food. May they be able to leave an inheritance to their children.

LORD, in your mercy, hear our prayer.

Based on Psalm 17:8-14

Anxiety

LORD, help your people not to worry about the wicked or envy those who do wrong. For you have said those who do wrong are like grass; they will soon shrivel like grass clippings and wilt like cut flowers in the sun. Instead, enable your people to trust in you and do good. Then, by your grace and mercy, they will live safely in the land and prosper. LORD, may your people take delight in you, and as they do that, give them their hearts' desires. May they commit everything that is happening to you, LORD. Help them to trust you and to be confident that you will help them. LORD, make their innocence radiate like the dawn and the justice of their cause to shine like the noonday sun.

LORD, in your mercy, strengthen your people.

Based on Psalm 37:1-6

Cry for help

O LORD, we cry out to you and will keep on pleading day by day. O LORD, why do you seem to turn a deaf ear? Why do you make yourself scarce? Your people stand helpless and desperate before the recent terrors. Fierce anger has overwhelmed them. Terrors have paralyzed them. Troubles swirl around them like floodwaters all day long. Sorrows surround them on every side. Their companions and loved ones have been taken away. Darkness is their closest friend. LORD, stand with them and give them hope.

LORD, have mercy on them.

Based on Psalm 88:13-18

Danger

LORD, see how the wicked wait in ambush for the godly, looking for an excuse to harm them. LORD, do not let the wicked succeed or let the godly be condemned when they are put on trial. Don't abandon the godly, but help them wait with hope in you, LORD. May they travel steadily along your path. Honor the godly by providing them with a safe place. May they live to see the wicked destroyed. They have seen wicked and ruthless people acting like tyrants, but when they look again, may those wicked people be gone! Though the godly search for them, may the wicked truly be gone! Pay close attention to the innocent, decent people, and give them a future as peacemakers.

LORD, in your mercy, hear our prayer.

Based on Psalm 37:32-37

Despair

*L*ORD, we pray for those who are frustrated and famished. They try one thing after another, but when nothing works, they get angry with you and their leaders. Wherever they look, they see trouble and anguish and despair. Their tragic circumstances have thrown them into the darkness and left them with nothing. Let these people who are walking in darkness see the great light of hope in you. For those who find themselves in a land of deep darkness, may your light shine.

LORD, in your mercy, hear our prayer.

Based on Isaiah 8:21-22, 9:2

False pretenses

*L*ORD, we see leaders who seem to worship you. They participate in all the ceremonies, the more pomp the better! But you want them to stop bringing their meaningless gifts; their offerings disgust you because you know their hearts and know these celebrations are all sinful and false. You want no more of their pious meetings. You hate their celebrations and festivals, as they are a burden to you. You cannot stand them! So, LORD, when they lift up their hands in prayer, do not look.

Though they offer many prayers, do not listen, for their hands are covered with the blood of innocent victims.

Instead, cause them to wash themselves and be clean! May they get their sins out of your sight and give up their evil ways. May they learn to do good, seek justice, help the oppressed, defend the cause of orphans, and fight for the rights of widows.

LORD, you have offered forgiveness if they repent. You promise that though their sins are like scarlet, you will make them as white as snow. Though they are red like crimson, you will make them as white as wool. If they will only obey you, they will know true success. But if they turn away and refuse to listen, they will be devoured by their enemies.

LORD, you have spoken. Change their hearts!

LORD, in your mercy, hear our prayer.

Based on Isaiah 1:12-20

God's faithfulness

LORD GOD All-Powerful, who is like you? LORD, when people lose hope because of the trials they face, may they remember that you are powerful and completely trustworthy. You rule the mighty oceans and calm the waves when they become unruly. Your arm has great power. Your hand is strong; your right hand is ready to act. Your kingdom is built on what is right and fair. Love and truth are in all you do. LORD, let those losing hope live in the light of your presence. Then, may those who praise you find joy in your name and in your righteousness, regardless of their circumstances.

LORD, in your mercy, hear our prayer.

Based on Psalm 89:8-9, 13-16

Justice

God, you have said that at the time you have planned, you will bring justice against the wicked. The proud have been warned to stop their boasting! You have told the wicked not to brag! They must not raise their weapons so proudly or speak with such arrogance. LORD, you alone judge; you decide who will rise and who will fall. Now, O God, break the strength of the wicked, and increase the power of the godly.

LORD, in your mercy, hear our prayer.

Based on Psalm 75:2,4,5,7,10

Loneliness

*L*ORD, when people feel that all have deserted them, may they remember that you are always there. They cannot ever get away from your Spirit, nor can they run away from you. If they go up to the heavens, you are there. If they lie down in the grave, you are there. If they rise with the sun in the east and settle in the west beyond the sea, you are there to guide them and to hold them with your right hand. Remind them that even the darkness is not dark to you—the night is as bright as the day, for day and night are the same to you.

LORD, in your mercy, hear our prayer.

Based on Psalm 139:7-12

Oppression

*L*ORD, we pray for the oppressed. Answer us. Cause your suffering people to be bold by giving them the strength they need. You, LORD, are great because you care for the humble and recognize arrogant people from far away. Though your people are surrounded by troubles, preserve them from the anger of their enemies. Clench your fist against the angry enemies! By your power, please save your people and do not let go of those your hands have made.

LORD, in your mercy, hear our prayer.

Based on Psalm 138:3, 6-8

Peace

*L*ORD, mediate between nations and settle international disputes. Cause all the nations to turn their weapons of war into instruments of provision and their destructive tools into means of healing. May all wars stop and the need for military training come to an end. May the leaders of nations hear your invitation, "Come, and live in the light of the LORD!"

LORD, in your mercy, hear our prayer.

Based on Isaiah 2:4-5

Protection

O LORD, deliver those who trust in you from the plans of evil people. Protect them from those who are violent, who plan evil in their hearts and stir up trouble all day long. The wounds these criminals cause bite deep like the poisonous fangs of a snake.

O LORD, keep your people out of the hands of the

wicked, and protect them from those who are violent and are plotting against them. They may fear a home invasion or an attack on the streets. Evil people place traps all along the way in attempts to steal personal information so they can take illegally what you have provided.

I call to you, LORD, "You are our God!" Listen to the cries for help! O Sovereign LORD, you are the strong one who is able to keep your people safe and protect them in these situations.

LORD, do not let evil people have their way. Do not let their plans succeed; otherwise, they will never stop planning evil. May the righteous people you protect thank you, and may your people feel secure under your protection.

LORD, in your mercy, hear our prayer.

Based on Psalm 140:1-8, 13

Protection from terrorists

Protect people who are threatened by terrorist attacks, especially when they seem to be at their weakest. O LORD, strengthen them. Lead them to a place of safety; rescue them because you delight in them. Then may they delight in you. Save your people from their enemies. Pull them away from the grip of those who hate them. Save them from cruel people. Then your people can praise you, LORD, among the nations.

LORD, in your mercy, hear our prayer.

Based on Psalm 18:18-19, 48-49

Rebelliousness

O LORD, why do leaders continue to invite punishment by continuing to do evil? Must they rebel forever? Their minds are infected, and their hearts are failing to respond to you. They are battered from head to foot—covered with bruises, welts, and infected wounds—without any way to change, be healed or salve their consciences. Their countries lie in ruins and their towns are burned down. Foreigners plunder their fields before their eyes and destroy everything they see. Their beautiful cities stand abandoned as roofless, bullet-riddled, bombed-out buildings in helpless cities under siege.

LORD of Heaven's Armies, if you don't spare a few survivors, they will be wiped out like Sodom, or destroyed like Gomorrah!

LORD, in your mercy, hear our prayer.

Based on Isaiah 1:5-9

Rescue

*L*ORD, the fertile fields have become a wilderness. Towns crushed by fierce anger lie in ruins. Will you allow the whole land to be ruined? Relent, O LORD, and do not let the land be completely destroyed. Even so, the earth will mourn, and the heavens will be draped in black because of this disaster against your people. Will you come to their aid? Will you change the situation? At the noise of shooting and bombing, the people flee in terror. They are hiding in the bushes and running for the mountains. All the towns have been abandoned—not a person remains!

LORD, have mercy.

Based on Jeremiah 4:26-29

Restoration

*L*ORD, after all the hardships and suffering, we ask that you would restore the land. May the children flourish and grow strong. May the barns be filled with crops of every kind. May the flocks and herds multiply by the thousands, even tens of thousands, and trucks be loaded down with produce. May there be no enemy attacking these lands, no innocent people going into captivity, no people crying in alarm in the cities and towns. As we trust in you, may we live joyfully and give you praise for bringing peace.

LORD, in your mercy, hear our prayer.

Based on Psalm 144:12-15

Spiritual battles

LORD, we are human, but as believers in you, we don't wage war as others do. You have called us to use your mighty weapons, not worldly weapons, to knock down the strongholds of human reasoning and to destroy false arguments. Destroy every proud obstacle that keeps people from knowing you. Capture their rebellious thoughts and teach them to obey Christ. Help us to be faithful witnesses.

LORD, in your mercy, hear our prayer.

Based on 2 Corinthians 10:3-5

Tyrants

We look forward to that wonderful day when you, LORD, give your people rest from sorrow and fear, from slavery and chains. Overthrow the harsh dictators and authoritarian leaders. Destroy the tyrants. Yes, end their insolence. Crush their wicked power and break their evil rule. They have crushed many people with blows that wouldn't stop and established a violent rule of anger with torture and persecution without restraint. Remove these tyrants and allow the earth to be at rest and quiet. Then we can sing again!

LORD, in your mercy, hear our prayer.

Based on Isaiah 14:3-7

Violent people

LORD, we pray for those who plan to commit violence, that they will seek you while you can be found. Cause these people to abandon their violent ways of life. Banish from their minds the very thoughts of doing wrong! Let them turn to you, LORD, so you may lavishly forgive them.

LORD, in your mercy, hear our prayer.

Based on Isaiah 55:6-7

Wars to cease

*O*LORD, as I hear and see the news from so many places in the world, my heart writhes in pain! My heart pounds within me! I cannot keep quiet. Your people have heard the blast of enemy trumpets and the roar of battle cries. Waves of destruction roll over the land until it lies in complete desolation.
Suddenly, all homes are destroyed; in a moment, all buildings are crushed. How long must people look at the signal flares and listen to the sirens warning of danger?

LORD, in your mercy, hear our prayer and have compassion on all who live in war zones.

Based on Jeremiah 4:19-21

Topical Index

A

Abandonment	17
Accountability	36
Addiction	9
Aggression	105
Anxiety	105
Authorities	36

B

Brokenhearted	17

C

Care for our world	81
Children	12, 90, 97
Choices	37
Christ's example	90
Christlikeness	45
Comfort	61
Confession	10, 91
Cry for help	106

D

Danger	18, 107
Dark paths	92
Darkness	18
Decisions	12
Deliverance	81
Dependence	46
Despair	19, 51, 108
Direction	55
Disasters	20

Discouragement 20, 61
Distress 62
Drought 82

E

Earthquakes 82
Elderly 21
Encouragement 46
Endurance 22, 62, 63

F

Faithfulness 22, 47
Famine 83
False pretenses 108
Fear 23
Floods 83
Focus 52
Food supplies 84
Freedom 13, 23, 92

G

Generosity 24, 64
God's faithfulness 109
God's love 25
Godliness 48
Good Shepherd 26
Good shepherds 48
Guarding one's eyes 97
Guidance 49, 53, 56

H

Healing 98
Homelessness 64
Honesty 37
Hope 26, 65

I

Insights 49
Integrity 38

J

Judging rightly 38
Justice 39, 66, 110
Justice for persecutors 66

L

Living in the light 93
Loneliness 111
Loss of control 84
Love 67
Love for enemies 68
Loving the stranger 68

M

Mistreatment 69

N

New hearts 94

O

Obsession 99
One body in Christ 94
Opposition 69
Oppression 111
Outreach 50

P

Parents 99
Patience 56
Peace 112
Peace and safety 70
Perpetrators 14
Persecution 70

Plagues 85
Pornography 100
Prayer for peace 40
Predators 101
Protection 27, 40, 57, 112
Protection from terrorists 113
Provision 28, 53, 58
Punishment 101
Purity 41

R

Rebelliousness 86, 114
Refuge 72
Refugees 72
Reliance 29
Relief from drought 86
Renewal 50
Repentance 41, 43
Rescue 30, 42, 74, 87, 115
Respect 43
Restoration 28, 30, 74, 115
Retribution 75
Revenge 75

S

Safety 31, 76
Security 76
Seekers 31
Self-deceit 95
Self-deception 44
Sexual abuse 102
Shelter 32
Sinful desires 103

Sovereignty 77
Spiritual battles 116
Standing firm 77
Strength 32
Support 78

T

Tornadoes and hurricanes 87
Triumph 33
Trust 54, 59
Tyrants 117

U

Understanding the times 34

V

Victory 79
Violent people 117

W

Wars to cease 118
Wisdom 44

References

Holy Bible, New Living Translation, Second Edition
Copyright © 1996, 2004, Tyndale Charitable Trust. All rights reserved.
All rights reserved. No part of this book may be reproduced in any form without permission in writing from the publisher, except in the case of brief quotations embodied in critical articles or reviews.
Electronic Edition STEP Files Copyright © 2005, QuickVerse. All rights reserved.

The Message: The Bible in Contemporary Language
Copyright © 2002 by Eugene H. Peterson.
All rights reserved.
No part of this book may be reproduced in any form without permission in writing from the publisher, except in the case of brief quotations embodied in critical articles or reviews.
Electronic Edition STEP Files Copyright © 2005, QuickVerse. All rights reserved.

The Holy Bible, New Century Version
Original work copyright © 1987, 1988, 1991 by Word Publishing. All rights reserved.
All rights reserved. No part of this book may be reproduced in any form without permission in writing from the publisher, except in the case of brief quotations embodied in critical articles or reviews.

Electronic Edition STEP Files Copyright © 2005, QuickVerse. All rights reserved.

God's Word
Original work copyright © 1995 by God's Word to the Nations Bible Society.
All rights reserved. No part of this book may be reproduced in any form without permission in writing from the publisher, except in the case of brief quotations embodied in critical articles or reviews.
Electronic Edition STEP Files Copyright © 2005, QuickVerse. All rights reserved.

The Holy Bible, English Standard Version
Copyright © 2001 by Crossway Bibles, a division of Good News Publishers. All rights reserved.
All rights reserved. No part of this book may be reproduced in any form without permission in writing from the publisher, except in the case of brief quotations embodied in critical articles or reviews.
Electronic Edition STEP Files Copyright © 2005,

QuickVerse. All rights reserved.

Other books by Leoma Gilley

The Still Small Voice of Love: A journey into a deeper relationship with Jesus
In this thought and prayer-provoking devotional, author Leoma Gilley leads readers by example as she explores Scripture and listens for God's responses. Readers are not only welcomed into Leoma's heart, but they also see the heart of Jesus in His intimate responses to her fears, needs, questions, and longings. After each devotional, readers are prompted to follow the Lectio Divina method of Scriptural study to expand and deepen their own personal relationships with Jesus Christ.

An Autosegmental Approach to Shilluk Phonology (SIL International and the University of Texas at Arlington Publications in Linguistics, Vol 103)

Every Day But Not Some, Glimpses Into the Everyday Lives of Sudanese
Reports about the Sudan are often critical and harsh, and it is easy to equate the people of the Sudan with their government's policies. By contrast, the stories in Every Day But Not Some offer a more positive view of what life is like for the ordinary Sudanese. The author spent

22 years in Sudan and draws from a vast range of relationships and experiences to tell the untold side of the individual people and cultures of the Sudan. This collection of stories reveals how learning another culture is rather like walking around in an unfamiliar house in the dark. You don't know where anything is until you bump into it, sometimes gently, sometimes painfully. All the while, you are desperately looking for a light switch in hopes of being able to see more clearly. Here is a candid, entertaining and informative look at life in the Sudan.

www.ingramcontent.com/pod-product-compliance
Lightning Source LLC
Chambersburg PA
CBHW021447070526
44577CB00002B/298